Topgrading®
101

Avoid Costly Mis-Hires

Dr. Brad Smart

Topgrading 101: Avoid Costly Mis-Hires   Dr. Brad Smart

Brad's Topgrading methods helped us maximize talent at GE.
> —Jack Welch, author of **Winning** and former Chairman,
> General Electric

Topgrading is the definitive manual for becoming an A player and for recognizing those traits in others.
> —Larry Bossidy, author of **Execution** and former Chairman,
> Honeywell

In the fight against cardiovascular disease and stroke, Topgrading helped us raise an additional $50 million over the previous year. Topgrading has saved lives.
> —Cass Wheeler, former CEO,
> American Heart Association

Brad and three of his team have all conducted Topgrading workshops for our managers, and all four received top ratings.
> —Kevin Silva, SVP Human Resources,
> Argo Group

Of all the changes I've made to improve our company, none has been more important than Topgrading.
> —Jon A. Boscia, former Chairman & CEO,
> Lincoln National Corporation

If you read it with the right kind of attention, *Topgrading* is the most important book ever written.
> —Pasquale Scopelliti
> *Recruiter* magazine

At American Power Conversion (APC), Topgrading has dramatically increased our success hiring high performers. Our commitment to the Topgrading process is greater than ever!
> —Andrew Cole, Senior Vice President Human Resources,
> American Power Conversion

Topgrading must be a continuous process of identifying and developing top talent to enhance overall organizational vitality.
> —Bill Conaty, Sr., VP Human Resources,
> General Electric Company

MarineMax is a huge fan of Brad Smart's Topgrading system. We began the process in 2002 and we're totally convinced Topgrading has significantly improved our bottom line.
> —William H. McGill, Chairman & CEO,
> MarineMax Inc.

About the Author

Dr. Smart is an internationally renowned management psychologist and consultant to many Global 500 companies. Brad completed his Ph.D. in Industrial Psychology at Purdue University, entered consulting, and after two years launched Smart & Associates, Inc., based in the Chicago area.

Topgrading: How Leading Companies Win by Hiring, Coaching, and Keeping the Best People is Brad's fourth book, typically #1 of over 1,400 books in its category. In 2008 *Topgrading for Sales: World-Class Methods to Interview, Hire, and Coach Top Sales Representatives* was released. In 1997 Brad and son Geoff, CEO of ghSMART, published the first article on Topgrading. Geoff is co-author of The New York Times bestseller, **Who**.

Brad is generally regarded as the world's most experienced executive interviewer and coach, having conducted over 6,500 chronological Topgrading Interviews in over 200 companies. Advisor to CEOs of leading companies, Brad was described in a front-page Wall Street Journal profile as "probing the executive minds—the software of business." He has been featured on CNN and in numerous publications including Fortune, Inc., and Chief Executive. His Topgrading Interview has been embraced as the best practice by companies including General Electric, Honeywell, Barclays, Johnson & Johnson, and American Heart Association.

Table of Contents

Trademarks and Copyrights

The marks Topgrading, Topgrader, Topgrade, and Topgrading Interview are registered marks of Bradford D. Smart and Geoffrey H. Smart. The copyrights to the Topgrading forms and guides, listed below, are owned by Smart & Associates, Inc.:

Topgrading Interview Guide

Topgrading Interview Guide for Sales Representatives

Topgrading Career History Form

Self-Administered Topgrading Interview Guide

Topgrading In-Depth Reference Check Guide

Topgrading In-Depth Reference Check Guide for Sales Representatives

Topgrading Interviewer Feedback Form

Topgrading Cost of Mis-Hires Form

Introduction

Whether you are an owner of a 10-person company, CEO of a Global 1,000 company, or a manager of a department, here's a scenario you probably can relate to:

You have a mixture of talent, and marginal performers cause you the most frustration. You'd like to spend more time helping your high performers achieve even more, but chronic low performers take up too much of your time, and they drag down the entire organization. You value talent… you *really* do, but you only have about 25% *high* performers. You try to coach the poorer performers, but… it rarely works. You occasionally replace one, but:

- recruiters don't send good enough candidates,

- the resumes of candidates are full of hype,

- your competency inter-views are not very reveal-ing,

- reference checks are gen-erally worthless,

> **Most companies hire *high* performers only 25% of the time.**

- too often the people hired disappoint you, and

- all those mis-hire are *very* costly.

Welcome to the club! Tens of thousands of case studies plus surveys of Global 1,000 companies show that only 25% of the people they hire and promote turn out to be *high* performers! Using common-place 50-minute round-robin competency (behavioral) interviews, 75% turn out to be disappointments. Sure, if managers are willing to live with "adequate" performers, most are "okay hires." But you know in your heart that "adequate" and "okay" are *not* good enough. You want true high performers, the best available, *for what you are willing to pay*. That means picking only the best people available for *every* job.

Chapter 4 of this book will highlight 12 common-sense Topgrading practices that have enabled thousands of managers and many leading companies to double or triple the number of...not just "adequate" performers...but *high* performers. Many Topgrading companies hire and promote high performers 90% of the time. Topgrading leaders state unequivocally that their companies are performing better because Topgrading tools have helped their managers pick better people. They're Topgraders.

What exactly is a "Topgrader?" We define Topgrader as a leader who hires or promotes high performers, *the top 10% of talent available for the compensation level*. So, if there are 10 qualified candidates waiting at your door and eager to take the job at the pay level you offer, you pick the #1 best candidate. If these are candidates for promotion again, you choose the best. Most companies have unsuccessful hiring and promoting methods because they usually pick just average or "adequate" candidates, not the best available for the pay.

What do high performers "look like?" Here's an abbreviated, though representative summary:

If you'd like to become a Topgrader, you can start today. This short book will teach you the essentials, which are easy to understand (but require some discipline and practice to achieve 90% success!).

At the risk of oversimplifying, Topgraders keep the commonplace round-robin competency interviews (which are better than "Tell me about yourself" interviews), but the achieve 75% - 90% hiring promoting success by:

> ## The "silver bullet" for 90% hiring and promoting success is the Topgrading Interview.

- nailing down *exactly* what they're looking for,

- developing *networks* who refer talented candidates,

- conducting very thorough, chronological *Topgrading Interviews*, and

- getting *candidates* to arrange personal reference calls with former bosses.

Topgrading Promoting methods are the same as Topgrading Hiring methods, but instead of external references, internal interviews are conducted with boss(es), peers, and subordinates.

The "silver bullet," by far the single most important skill assuring hiring and promoting success of 75%-90%, is the Topgrading Interview. Why? Because when you conduct a Topgrading Interview, you follow a "road map," an interview guide that helps you learn about every success, every failure, every key decision, and every key relationship… for every full time job. No wonder this interview is so revealing! There, you have it—some of the "secrets" to joining the Topgrading club.

Summary of Critical Competencies: Upper Level Manager

	HIGH PERFORMER	ADEQUATE	LOW PERFORMER
Overall Talent Level	Top 10% of those available at this salary level	65th-89th percentile available at this salary level	Below the 65th percentile available at this salary level
Problem Solving	A "quick study:" able to rapidly perform complex analyses.	Smart; "average" insight.	Has difficulty coping with complex situations.
Leadership	Executes needed change; highly adaptive and able to inspire the organization.	Favors modest change, so there is lukewarm "followership."	Prefers the status quo; lacks credibility so people don't follow.
Passion	Very high energy level; fast paced; 55 (+) hour work weeks (plus home email); driven to succeed.	Motivated; energetic at times; 50-54 hour work weeks.	Dedicated; inconsistent pace; 40-49 hour work weeks.
Resourceful-ness	Impressive ability to find ways over, around, or through barriers; can-do attitude.	Occasionally finds a solution; relies on others to "figure it out."	Defeated by obstacles; constantly "delegates" to bosses.
Topgrading	Selects high performers and employees with potential; redeploys chronic underperformers.	Selects a few high performers.	Selects mostly underperformers; tolerates mediocrity.
Coaching	Successfully counsels each team member to turbo-boost performance and personal/career growth.	Performs annual performance reviews; "spotty" coaching.	Inaccessible, hypercritical, stingy with praise; late/shallow with feedback.
Team Building	Creates focused, collaborative, results-driven teams.	May want teamwork but does not make it happen.	Drains energy from others; actions prevent synergy.
Track Record	Consistently excellent performance.	Meets some (not all) key constituency expectations.	Sporadically meets expectations.
Integrity	"Iron-clad."	Generally honest.	"Bends the rules."
Communication	Excellent oral/written skills.	Average oral/written skills.	Mediocre.

Chapter 1

Why Picking Talent is Your Most Pressing, Frustrating Challenge

"Nothing matters more in winning than getting the right people on the field. All the clever strategies and advanced technologies in the world are nowhere near as effective without great people to put them to work."

—Jack Welch, *Winning*

I don't want to preach to the choir, because anyone reading this book is a member of the "choir" of talent-oriented leaders. You know talent is all-important, but if you are like most managers, you are frustrated with too many costly mis-hires. You've read the survey results—when CEOs or any managers convene, they say "picking the right people" is their biggest headache, most pressing problem, their most frustrating challenge. Why? Because despite the importance of hiring high performers, most managers pick them only 25% of the time.

Let me give you a little different slant on this—where I'm coming from. I've conducted 65,000 face-to-face case studies that have made it glaringly obvious that the single most important factor in a manager's success is the *talent* of the team assembled.

I wish academicians would study this scientifically, but from these 65,000 case studies, the conclusion seems crystal clear: Create a team of high performers and you're likely to succeed, but keep a lot of low performers and you're apt to fail.

"Duh," you say. Of course it's possible to have a mediocre team that produces great results, because you have a monopoly, patent protection, colossally weak competitors, or lobbyists who (ahem) give you some "competitive advantage." And it's possible to have all high performers but your team fails, because the CEO insists on the wrong strategy, the organization culture is in-bred and lame, someone steals your IP, or markets dry up with a burp in the economy. But you know that most of the time, talent wins.

> **Create a team of high performers and you're likely to succeed, but keep a lot of low performers and you're apt to fail.**

For years I've studied the frustration associated with hiring low performers. Every manager experiences that pain! For example, one of our studies showed the average cost of a management mis-hire to be 15 times base salary. Chapter 4 provides additional documentation of how frustrating, painful, and costly it is to mis-hire people.

Why it *Was* Smart For You to Keep Some "Adequate" Performers

For most managers *not* exposed to Topgrading, all that frustration, wasted time, lessened job performance, and high costs of mis-hires are very understandable. What?? Yes… let me explain.

Suppose your mixture of talent is similar to what thousands of managers I've interviewed described in their teams.

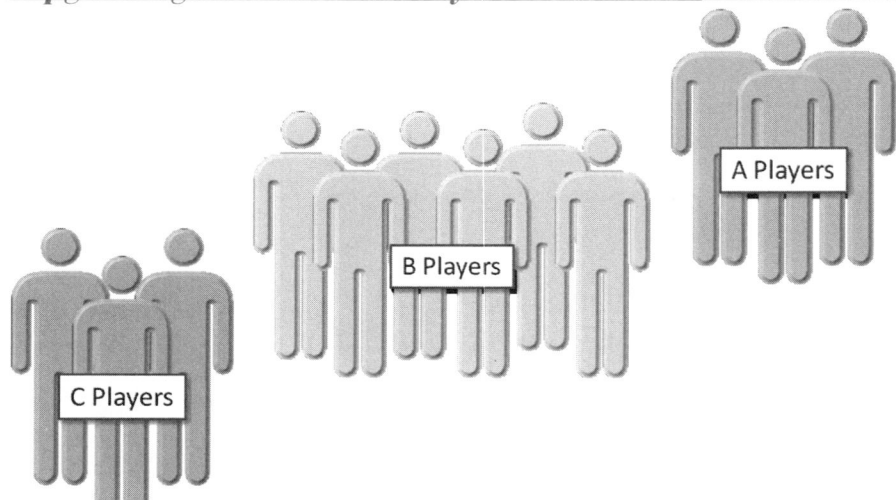

If your track record is typical, and only 25% of the people you re-place turn out to be high performers, it would be too risky for you to replace disappointing but "adequate" performers. You are very sure they are not as good as the top 10% of talent available, for exactly the same pay, but if your hiring 'batting average' is only 25%, then there is a 50% chance your replacements will be no better than your current "adequate" performers. And, to make things worse, there is a 25% chance your replacements will be *worse—low* performers.

So it was (and still is) smart for you to give your high performers a lot of support and coaching. And it was (and still is) smart to replace your chronic low performers, the ones that cause the biggest prob-lems and keep you awake at night. And it was (until you learned about Topgrading) smart to retain your "adequate" performers be-cause you were only 25% successful picking high performers.

Aah... but this scene changes when you're a Topgrader. When 75% - 90% of the people you hire turn out to be high performers, it's smart and rational to replace not only low performers, but those "adequate" performers. To drive home this point, please take this short mind-teasing quiz:

Topgrading Mind Teaser

Q: If you inherit 10 low performers and want to re-place all 10 with high performers, how many peo-ple do you have to hire if your hiring success is 25%?

A: 40... You hire 40 people.

Q: How many do you have to fire?

A: 40... the 10 you inherited plus the 30 you mis-hired.

Any manager would be nuts to fire 40 people when the team is only 10 people. The revolving door would be chaos!

Q: How many would a Topgrader have to hire, with a 90% success rate?

A: 11

Q: How many would the Topgrader have to fire?

A: One... which gives the Topgrader a 30:1 advantage over the non-Topgrader. Thirty mis-hires versus one mis-hire!

This little game is better than any drug for reducing your frustration and the costs of mis-hires. That sounds more flippant than it should. Topgraders experience less frustration and lower costs than others, because they enjoy much more success hiring and promoting high performers.

Chapter 2

Why Commonplace Hiring Methods are Poor

> "The ability to make good decisions regarding people is one of the last reliable sources of competitive advantage, since very few companies are good at it."
>
> —Peter Drucker

Every week one or more companies supplement their existing hiring and promoting methods by embracing Topgrading. Why? Because the hiring and promoting practices embraced by most companies are so inadequate; they are demonstrably mediocre at picking high performers. Here are some data points:

- I met with just the #1 human resources executives of <u>Global 100</u> companies, and they completed a survey showing 80% of the managers they hire turn out to be disappointments. And they said that 75% of the people promoted turn out to be disappointments. How can Human Resources be respected, with such appalling results?

- <u>McKinsey Quarterly</u> (January '08) published another article ("Making Talent a Strategic Priority") in The War for Talent series, showing how the image of HR is mediocre. Line managers say the so-called "best practices" of HR just don't work, and they complain that HR is not accountable for *quality* of hires. Worse yet, in the past 10 years the image of HR has *declined.*

For HR to improve its image, Topgrading can help. It's the easiest way I know for HR to become *highly* valued.

- Two hundred CEOs reported to us that they felt they got their money's worth from executive search firms only 21% of the time.

- On a conference call the head of HR at a pharmaceuticals company told me they use round-robin competency interviews and achieve "97.5% hiring success." Skeptical, I asked how the measurement is done, and he said, "The hiring manager is sent an email 30 days after the person is hired, asking, 'Does the person hired have the skills to do the job?' It's a yes/no question, with 97.5% responding yes." Great! Why not just ask if the person recently hired has a pulse? I asked, "What percent of managers hired turn out to be the high performers expected—and the only other category is mis-hire?" "Oh," he said, "probably only 20% turn out to be high performers, and 80% are mis-hires."

- In 2010 a leading human resources software company, Peopleclick Authoria, began offering the 12 Topgrading steps in its Talent methods.

- I was Special Advisor to an <u>American Productivity and Quality Center</u> study (published in 2008) in which 19 companies participated as case studies, sponsors, or both. Only one company—a Topgrading company, Lincoln Financial Group—stood out for both measuring success hiring and promoting people. And Lincoln's success using Topgrading Hiring and Promoting: 90% high performers.

- Go to any of the human resources benchmarking company web sites, and see if they measure percent of high performers hired or promoted. Only one we know of—Peopleclick Authoria. HR frequently measures hiring costs and time to fill jobs…

they hire the wrong people 75% of the time, but they do it in-expensively and quickly! What's wrong with that picture?

Business today is run on metrics. Everything under the sun is measured... *except* what is arguably the single most important factor, quality of people hired and promoted. Companies have embraced TQM, Six Sigma, re-engineering, a zillion financial metrics, Toyota methods, lean manufacturing, dashboards, and Black Belts, but only Topgraders systematically measure quality of those hired/promoted.

Why? I believe poor hiring is so widespread that the business world suffers from widespread self-deception. No one wants to acknowledge that mediocre hiring/promoting is the huge pile of elephant poop stinking up results. It's like steroid use in baseball: it's wide-spread and everyone knew it but no one wanted to face it.

> **Bad hiring is the huge pile of elephant poop, stinking up results.**

Well, maybe it's time to "face it," to confront the reality that hiring practices in most companies are terribly ineffective.   Topgraders "face it."   They rigorously measure quality of hire and adopt methods that clearly improve hiring success... oftentimes achieving 90% high performers hired/promoted.

Keep Commonplace Best Practices... But Don't Expect Better Than 25% High Performers Hired/ Promoted Without Adding the Topgrading Interview

What are the typical "best practices" of global companies, Fortune 1,000 companies, and smaller companies that copy big companies?

- A job analysis is conducted...

- that produces a (*vague*) job description...

- with perhaps six competencies (out of dozens that are crucial for success) identified…

- that are investigated through six (*easily faked*) round-robin competency (behavioral) interviews, each 50-minutes long, with verification of conclusions through...

- reference checks… which are marginally useful because most companies don't allow managers to take reference calls, and besides, reference sources are provided by *candidates* (who "salt the mines" with *buddies*).

Look at the case studies on the web sites for companies selling competency (behavioral) interviewing approaches. Too many of those case studies simply show that managers are happy with the interview training but give little data about the *quality* of hires. Some case studies suggest there are more "adequate" performers hired rather than low performers—okay, that's good—but I haven't seen one case study from any company selling competency interviews that credibly shows a significant increase in *high* performers hired.

In all my books I recommend keeping the job analysis, job description (with some improvements), and even the round-robin competency

Keep competency interviews but add the Topgrading Interview.

interviews I've criticized; talented candidates want to talk to more than Topgrading interviewers, and competency (behavioral) questions are better than idle chit chat. But to improve from 25% high performers hired to 80% or 90% success, add the Topgrading Interview.

Chapter 3

How Topgrading Hiring/Promoting Methods
Became the Best

"No company can expect to beat the competition unless it has the best human capital and promotes these people to pivotal positions. *Topgrading* is the definitive manual for becoming a high performer and for recognizing those traits in others."

—Larry Bossidy, author of
Execution, and former Chairman, Honeywell

Topgrading methods are regarded by many respected leaders to be the best because they:

- require intellectually honest measurement of *quality* of hires/ promotions,

- set the bar high... with the total focus on hiring/promoting people who turn out to be *high* performers, not just "adequate" performers, and

- have proven, again and again, to double and triple hiring success. You'll read case studies in which companies improved from 25% to even 90% high performers hired, and please note: the CEOs of the case studies signed off on the results published, and the names of the companies are revealed.

Topgrading 101: Avoid Costly Mis-Hires   Dr. Brad Smart

How did these methods evolve? For over three decades I've been on a mission to discover methods that achieve the one most important goal: hiring/promoting *high* performers. Quality is most important to you, too, or you would not be reading this!

For all of my career I've studied what companies and individual managers have done that worked and what didn't work. Early in my career I asked companies to tell me how successful my recommended candidates turned out. Sounds like bragging, but when I achieved 90%+ high performers hired/promoted, and the company I worked for achieved far less with tests and 1 ½ hour interviews, I launched Smart & Associates, Inc.

How did I get the results? In my singleminded quest to achieve 90%+ high performers hired, I started out with a competency interview approach, trying to elicit behaviors that would reflect key competencies. Forgive my English, but I knew I was being "BSed." So I began asking candidates everything important about every job. Gradually I developed the most thorough interview approach—the Topgrading Interview. Other chronological interview methods were around, but I turbo-boosted the thoroughness and added a "truth serum."

As Mark Sutton, head of UBS commented, "How can a bunch of short competency interviews compete with the systematic and much more thorough Topgrading Interview?" They can't!

In the 1980s, Jack Welch hired Smart & Associates, Inc. to improve General Electric's hiring and promoting methods, but Welch was determined to *not* be so reliant on outside Topgrading professionals to pick winners. Together Welch and I figured out the methods and training so that GE managers and HR professionals could approximate the 90% success of Topgrading professionals. When Jack approved two interviewers, the Tandem Topgrading Interview, GE's success shot up.

Topgrading 101: Avoid Costly Mis-Hires   Dr. Brad Smart

With GE the most respected company in the world, and Jack Welch named "CEO of the Century," other leading companies wanted to double and triple their success hiring and promoting people. Larry Bossidy (Honeywell), and Cass Wheeler (American Heart Association) are among the CEOs who early on embraced Topgrading.

Jack Welch, Former CEO, General Electric, author, *Winning*

As far as I know, the only published case studies of hiring processes, where *high* performer is the standard, are Topgrading case studies. In the 2005 version of *Topgrading: How Leading Companies Win by Hiring, Coaching, and Keeping the Best People,* representative Topgrading case studies across a variety of companies are provided, many of which achieved 90% *high* performers hired or promoted using Topgrading methods.

Larry Bossidy, Former CEO, Honeywell, author, *Execution*

New case studies are popping up all the time! Microsoft and Johnson & Johnson launched Topgrading programs, and Barclays is rolling out Topgrading throughout the world. Two of the top global real estate management companies, Jones Lang LaSalle and DTZ, are Topgraders. So are Argo (global insurance) and Roundy's (retailer).

Cass Wheeler, Former CEO, American Heart Association, author, *Have a Heart*

Smart & Associates, Inc. has an "exclusive" contract with Peopleclick Authoria (PCA), the HR software company, to not permit its

CASE STUDIES FOR 2005 *Topgrading*

	New Case Studies	Revisited Case Studies
Large Companies	Lincoln Financial	General Electric
	Hillenbrand	HEB
	Hayes Lemmerz	Nielsen
	Barclays Capital	
Mid-sized Companies	Marine Max	Dominick's
	American Heart Association	
Small Companies	Virtual Technology	
	ghSMART	

competitors to embed Topgrading tools in their software serving clients. PCA wants to not just handle the technology in recruiting and other HR functions, but offer clients the best hiring and promoting methods. So, PCA is now the only HR software company to offer clients all of the 12 Topgrading steps described in this book, plus learning videos and other tools. And PCA has a partnership with Mercer, so Global 1000 companies are hearing about Topgrading from two leading HR companies.

Kennametal, a $2.5 billion supplier of tooling, engineered components and advanced materials used in production processes, launched Topgrading by having managers participate in Topgrading workshops, and Kevin Walling, VP & Chief HR Officer, said, "Kennametal has used the concepts of Topgrading for over five years now…

resulting in significantly greater success in hiring the **right** person for the job across the globe."

Topgrading ROI

Unlike any other hiring approach, Topgrading is trying to produce analyses of ROI for entire companies. Most companies simply conclude that if they avoid one costly mis-hire, their ROI is high and if half the managers avoid one mis-hire in the next five years, Topgrading costs will be paid for... for a hundred years!

In *Topgrading for Sales: World-Class Methods to Interview, Hire, and Coach Top Sales Representatives* (Portfolio, 2008), co-author Greg Alexander contributed a conservative scenario that would provide an increase in shareholder value of $75 million... for a $200 million company.   Here are the base financial assumptions for a company with 400 sales people:[1]

Pre-Topgrading

Shares Outstanding......................10,0000,000
Share Price $22
Earnings Per Share.....................................$1
P/E Ratio 22
Market Cap $220M

---

1 The source of the financial ratio data is the 541 companies according to Yahoo Finance that are in the Information Technology sector with revenues greater than $100M based on 2006 financial performance.

If this company reduced its mis-hire rate from 40% to 20% in just the sales area, their financials could look like this after just one year:

Post-Topgrading
Shares Outstanding......................**10,0000,000**
Share Price **$26.40**
Earnings Per Share...................**$1.2**
P/E Ratio **22**
Market Cap **$264M**

Pages of data are provided which support the data above and lead us to this conclusion:

> *Through the P/E leverage, Topgrading produces a 20% shareholder revenue increase, generating over $44M in shareholder wealth in the first year, and a total of 34% shareholder return—16% compound annual growth rate— creating $75M in shareholder wealth, in the first two years of Topgrading deployment.*

As more companies measure quality of hires and study methods that improve both quality of hire and the real business results from improving hiring, the more Topgrading methods stand out.

I hope you appreciate the fact that Topgrading methods are not mysterious, but they are unique in their emphasis on hiring high performers and honestly measuring hiring success. And in the next chapter you'll learn the abbreviated version of key Topgrading methods and, I hope, help you immediately hire and promote better.

Chapter 4

Twelve Topgrading Best Practices

"Those who build great companies understand that the ultimate throttle on growth for any great company is not markets, or technology, or competition, or products. It is the one thing above all others; the ability to get and keep enough of the right people."

—Jim Collins, author of *Good to Great*

Here it is… sort of the Cliff Notes version of Topgrading. Entire books, articles, and video tapes have been created on the 12 steps in this abbreviated Topgrading manual, but there is enough "meat" here to enable you to immediately hire and promote better performers. You probably will want to do better than just "improve;" you probably want to achieve 90% success. Hey, first things first!

This chapter focuses on Topgrading Hiring. But remember, Topgrading Promoting steps are different only in that "reference checks" are internal rather than external.

What are Topgrading Hiring/Promoting Best Practices?

There are 12 Topgrading hiring steps, with "tweaks" for promoting, but the essential steps are:

- Ask candidates to complete the Topgrading Career History Form, with its "truth serum" that requests much more useful

 Career History Form

INSTRUCTIONS

Thank you for completing the Topgrading Career History Form. Please read these instructions carefully before completing the form.

1. In the Business Experience section, each letter (A, B, C, etc.) corresponds to a specific job. If, for example, your present employer is Acme Inc. and you have had three different jobs with Acme, then:

    A is your present job with Acme
    B is the next previous job at Acme, and
    C is your first job with Acme

    Please complete a section of this form (A, B, C, etc.) **for every job** where there was a change in your job title.

2. Begin with your present, or most recent, job and progress backward in time until you complete the form for your first full time job.

3. Understand that if you are applying for a job with a different employer, before a final job offer *you will probably be asked to arrange personal reference calls with supervisors and others you have worked with*. There are several reasons we ask you to do this:

    a) Your development. Candid, confidential insights of supervisors and others can be used to help you move smoothly into the next job and can help you create a powerful Individual Development Plan.
    b) Verification. Confidential reference calls with supervisors and others will add credibility to the information you have provided throughout the hiring process.
    c) Ease. It's difficult for us to get former supervisors and others to talk with us, but high performers CAN arrange for those personal discussions.

4. Please complete and return this form to the company that requested it within 3 business days.

information than supplied by resumes.

- Supplement 1-hour competency interviews with the chrono-logical Topgrading Interview, and for managerial jobs, use the Tandem Topgrading (2 interviewers) method. This is the most important Topgrading method, covering every success, failure, decision, key relationship, and appraisal by every boss.

- At the end of the Topgrading Interview, the interviewers decide whom they want to talk with and the candidate arranges the personal reference calls. Because candidates know they will have to arrange personal reference calls with bosses, they are … honest … in the interviews and in completing the Topgrading Career History Form.

Now let's press the re-set button and walk through all 12 of the Topgrading hiring steps.

Topgrading Hiring Step #1: Measure Hiring Success

Everyone knows that in business if something is important it has to be measured … or the results will never be achieved. But most companies do not measure success hiring and promoting people.

Topgrading uses two simple tools. One is percent high performers hired and promoted. Most companies estimate 25 – 30% high performers, 50% "adequate" but disappointing, and the rest … you know!

Topgrading® **Cost of Mis-Hires Form**©

Job title of person mis-hired or mis-promoted: _____

Dates person was in position: from_____ to _____

Reason for leaving:
Quit ___, Fired (or forced to resign) ___, Transferred ___, Demoted ___, Retired ___, Died ___, Other ___.

1. **Total costs in hiring the person:** $_____
   - Recruitment/search fees (any guarantee? if so, was money recovered?)
   - Outside testing, interviewing, record checking, physical exam
   - HR department time and administrative costs (for all candidates)
   - Travel costs (for all candidates, spouses, other executives traveling to meet candidate)
   - Time/expenses of non HR people (all candidates)
   - Relocation (moving household goods, purchasing house for candidate)

2. **Compensation:** (sum for all years person was in job) $_____
   - Base ($_____ × number of years)
   - Bonuses ("signing," performance, etc.) for all years
   - Stock options (realized for all years), benefits (insurance, 401k, etc.), car, clubs

3. **Maintaining person in job:** (sum for all years person was in job) $_____
   - Administrative assistant for all years
   - Office "rental" (incl. electricity, etc.) for all years
   - Furniture, computer, equipment, travel for all years
   - Training
   - Other "maintaining" costs

4. **Total severance:** $_____
   - Severance fee (salary, benefits, use of office), lawyer fees
   - Outplacement counseling fee
   - Costs in lawsuits caused by the person (EEOC, harassment, EPA, OSHA, etc.)
   - Administrative costs in separation, wasted time of people in separation

5. **Mistakes/Failures, missed and wasted business opportunities:** $_____
   (For example… drove a key customer away, impaired customer loyalty, launched three "dog" products)

6. **Disruption:** $_____
   (Costs of inefficiency in the organization, lower morale, lower productivity, impaired teamwork)

7. **Other:** $_____

8. **SUM OF ALL COSTS** (#1 through #7): $_____

9. **Estimated Value of Contributions** of the mis-hire: $_____
   (Even if a $50,000 per year store manager drove away customers and stole $1M, perhaps he contributed something — hired five excellent employees, came up with a merchandising idea worth $500K per year to the bottom line.)

10. **NET COST OF MIS-HIRE** (#8 – #9): $_____

"WASTED" Hours:
Number of additional hours you and others spent dealing with mis-hire's weak points — patching things up with customers, etc.   _____

The other tool is the <u>Topgrading Cost of Mis-Hires Form</u>. In a few minutes a team can conservatively estimate the costs of a typical mis-hire in any job. For mid-managers it's typically $400,000+ and for sales reps it's over $500,000.

Sales Representative
HIring Costs $23,500
Compensation $151,000

2010 © Smart & Associates, Inc.

Maintenance $14,000
Severance $25,000
Opportunity Costs $250,000
Disruption Costs $100,000
Total...$563,500

These two measurements produce emotional commitment, a feeling in the gut that we must improve our success hiring and promoting people.

Topgrading Hiring Step #2: Create a Job Scorecard

Exit interviews show that neither hiring managers nor candidates typically understand *enough* about the job to avoid confusion and, too often, poor performance. That's because job descriptions (containing responsibilities, budget, competencies) are *too vague.*

Topgrading Job Scorecard

Candidate Name	
Title	
Company Name	
Date	
Rating (High Performer, Adequate, Low Performer)	
Recommendations	

Key Accountabilities

	Accountabilities	Importance (H, M, L)	Rating and Comments
1	Revenue – Exceed annual revenue quota of $1.0M.	H	
2	Achieve 15% margin.	M	
3	Activities – Maintain an activity level of 7 in-person sales calls per week.	M	
4	Conversion – Build pipeline to quota ratio of 5:1	M	
5	Conversions – Sell each deal with an average selling price at or above company averages.	M	
6	Talent – Consistently rank in the top 20% of industry sales reps in total sales	H	
7	Time – Spend 240 selling days out of the fiscal year's 260 in the field with prospects.	M	

Topgrading companies know that costly mis-hires are avoided when one extra step is taken, and that is to nail down the **measurable accountabilities** that turn the confusing job description into a very clear **job scorecard**.

The job scorecard spells out everything that must be accomplished: *"Achieve these measurable accountabilities and you are an A player."*

Topgrading job scorecards include templates for something unique – color-coded competencies: green are competencies Topgrading professionals agree can be developed, red are almost impossible to change, and yellow are in-between. Note that the Job Scorecard has spaces to enter the Minimum Acceptable Rating and it has space to record Final Ratings, after all the interviews and reference checks. Below are 3 of the 50 competencies, color-coded.

COMPETENCIES (GREEN = RELATIVELY EASY TO CHANGE, YELLOW = HARDER TO CHANGE BUT DOABLE, RED = VERY DIFFICULT TO CHANGE)	DEFINITION	Minimum Acceptable Rating (5 = Excellent, 4 = Very Good, 3 = Good, 2 = Only Fair, 1 = Poor, N/A)	TANDEM INTERVIEWERS' RATING
INTELLECTUAL			
Judgment/Decision Making	Consistent logic, rationality & objectivity in decision making. Neither indecisive nor hip-shooter.		
Education	Meets formal & informal educational requirements. Exhibits continuous learning.		
PERSONAL			
Integrity	Iron clad. Does not ethically cut corners. Earns trust of co-workers. Puts organization above self interests.		

Topgrading Hiring Step #3: Recruit from Networks

"Floss daily." "Diversify your investments." And to recruit, call on your network of (a) high performers you know, and (b) "connectors,"

> ## "We recruit all day, every day, with everyone we meet."
> ## --Ann Drake, CEO DSC Logistics

who know a lot of high performers. All are obvious truths.

Every manager knows recruiting from Networks is much better than hiring recruiters or running ads, because it's **faster** (email them today, talk with high performers within days), **cheaper** (no recruiter fees), and **better** (candidates are pre-screened high performers).

Topgraders are using LinkedIn, Facebook, and email lists to recruit, because it works. Staying in touch with 100 high performers is time consuming, and social media can save you time.

For example, if you have a social media group for recruiting sales reps, and it includes top sales reps you've worked with and heard about, plus sales managers who know high performing sales reps, you can stay in touch by simultaneously sending all of them an interesting article on new technology that helps sales reps (or whatever) and calling them a couple of times each year.

Topgrading Hiring Step #4: Screen Candidates with the Topgrading Career History Form

Every book on how to get a job teaches C players how to write an A player resume. Every HR professional knows how exasperating it is to spend hours in interviews and finally realize that the candidate's resume was full of hype, and omitted many negative facts.

The Topgrading Career History Form saves a lot of time and, more importantly, gets the best candidates in the door for interviews. It

looks like an application form (and licensees can make changes on it, with my permission), but it is a powerful pre-screening tool because it contains:

- a "truth serum," a statement that just before a job offer the *candidate* must arrange personal reference calls with former bosses, peers, and subordinates. C player candidates drop out. Good! A players are eager to arrange those calls

- requests for full job dates (so short jobs can't be hidden), estimated boss ratings of overall performance (for every job), estimated boss ratings of key competencies, true reasons for leaving employers ... and much more.

Topgrading Hiring Step #5: Conduct a Telephone Screening Interview

Companies vary widely in this step, but the common interest is this: When you invite candidates in for interviews, and those candidates wash out, you've wasted a lot of money and time. The Topgrading Career History Form (Step #4) is a powerful pre-screening tool. But Topgrading companies typically find they effectively reject some more weak candidates in the Telephone Screening interview.

The Telephone Screening Interview Guide suggests explaining the job in more detail, and if the candidate is still interested, take 45 minutes to ask about the most recent 2 jobs (successes, failures, key decisions, key relationships, estimated ratings by bosses), reasons for job changes, goals, and some competency questions.   It's "Topgrading Interview Lite," and it moves quickly since the completed Topgrading Career History Form is at hand.

For technical jobs, there sometimes is a series of technical questions or even a separate phone screen interview.

The combination of steps #4 and #5 results in almost every candidate who subsequently comes in for interviews is Very Good or Excellent.

Topgrading Hiring Step #6: Conduct a Series of Competency Interviews

Most companies, including most Global 100 companies, rely *mostly* on competency (behavioral) interviews to screen candidates, and the result is only 25% high performers hired or promoted. Topgraders know that Step #7, the Topgrading Interview, produces 1000% more valid insights into candidates than competency interviews.

More than 100 books on job hunting advise candidates, including C player candidates, how to *fake* competency interviews. It's easy – any managerial job requires teamwork, so "Think of the time you were a great team player and practice exaggerating your teamwork skills. And you'll be asked about a time you were not such a good team player – so think of a time, or make one up and say it occurred long ago, and explain that you were actually pretty good and since then you've become great." Heh, heh. Outplacement counselors provide the same sort of "heh, heh" advice to conceal negatives and hype positives.

So why conduct competency interviews? Five one-hour interviews focused on one or two key competencies will produce some useful insights, but also, as Tamela Seldess points out, those interviews give A player candidates the opportunity to meet more people and ask more questions.

Topgrading Hiring Step #7: Conduct the Topgrading Interview

This is the "silver bullet" of hiring. Every manager we know of achieving 90% hiring or promoting success, conducts the Topgrading Interview, using the Topgrading Interview Guide.

The Topgrading Interview is a chronological interview, starting with the educational years and coming forward to the present, and con-

cluding with the usual sections on Self-Appraisal and Plans and Goals for the Future.

The Topgrading Interview Guide is 30 pages long, but is not as onerous as that sounds. The "guts" of the Topgrading Interview is asking candidates 16 basic questions about each job and that means you learn about every success and accomplishment, every failure and mistake, every key relationship, every boss, and estimated ratings by every boss.

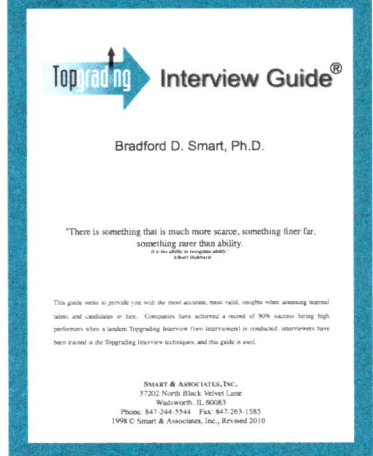

You won't believe this: thousands of Topgrading managers, using the Guide, gain deep and accurate insights into 50 competencies. (No, that's not a typo – 50!)

In every one of our quarterly Topgrading Workshops attendees admit that they did not believe they could accurately rate a candidate on more than a few competencies, and definitely not 50, and they "way down deep" did not believe they could ever achieve 90% hiring success.

But day two of the workshop they do it all – analyze a completed Topgrading Career History Form, conduct a four-hour Tandem Topgrading Interview, write a report, and provide feedback and coaching, with developmental recommendations, to their workshop interviewee. *Doing it all* is crucial, because afterwards there are high fives among interviewers and interviewees, and the workshop attendees *know* they can do it because … they did it!

It's like a golf clinic for two days and on the second day you shoot 15 strokes better than your best score. (Trouble is, that never happens in golf … but it does happen with Topgrading!)

"What?" you say, "It's too time consuming for two interviewers to take three hours for a chronological interview." Let's run some numbers. Suppose you calculate a mis-hire costs $400,000 and you waste 200 hours on each mis-hire. And suppose you mis-hire three sales reps, and fire all three, before hiring a good one. After all, your hiring success is average—one success in four. Your results are typical for sales managers. You waste $1.2 million plus 600 hours with your three mis-hires. Six hours for a tandem interview with 90% success would, according to your own calculations, save $1.2 million and about 600 hours.

The sentence that makes absolutely zero sense is, "I don't have time for a three-hour tandem interview that will at least triple my chances of hiring a high performer… but I can afford to waste $1.2 million and over 400 hours."

Below is a sample page of the 30-page Topgrading Interview Guide:

Topgrading Interview Guide (sample page)

JOB #1 FORM
This form is for the first full time job (usually following college).

1. _____
   Employer   Starting date (mo./yr.)   Final (mo./yr.)

   _____
   Location   Type of business

2. Title _____

   ⎡ Base $_____ ⎤   ⎡ Base $_____ ⎤
   ⎢ Bonus $_____ ⎥   ⎢ Bonus $_____ ⎥
3. Salary (Starting) ⎣ Other $_____ ⎦ Salary (Final) ⎣ Other $_____ ⎦

4. Expectations _____

5. Responsibilities/Accountabilities _____

6. "Found" (Major Challenges) _____

7. Successes/Accomplishments (How achieved?) _____

8. Failures/Mistakes (Why?) (Do differently?) _____

9. Most Enjoyable _____

10. Least Enjoyable _____

11. Talent _____

SUPERVISOR

12. _____
    Supervisor's Name   Title

    _____
    Where Now   Permission to Contact?

13. Appraisal of Supervisor His/Her Strengths _____

    His/Her Shortcomings _____

14. Best guess as to what he/she really felt at that time were your strengths, weak points, and overall performance rating:

STRENGTHS	WEAK POINTS

Overall Performance Rating _____

15. Other important decisions or relationships _____

The Topgrading Interview Guide greatly simplifies the inherently complex interview process.

Topgrading Hiring Step #8: Interviewers Receive Feedback and Coaching

Topgrading 101: Avoid Costly Mis-Hires   Dr. Brad Smart

In almost every study, perhaps including surveys you've conducted in your company, new hires say their interviewers were not very good. Most managers typically attend one 1-day interviewing workshop, and that's it – they never receive further training or coaching. When they interview, they talk too much, "lead the witness," fail to take notes, forget to use the candidate's name and … you get it.

Managers in Topgrading companies attend Topgrading workshops, but a key to continued improvement is Step #8 – immediately following the Tandem Topgrading Interview, the interviewers take just five minutes and give each other feedback, using a checklist of 40 interviewing techniques they learned in the workshop. Basically they tell each other, "Of the 40 interviewing techniques, you were particularly good at these (five), and you could improve at these (three)." Over time the interviewers get better and better. After conducting over 6,500 in-depth, chronological interviews I still mess up; people sit in on my interviews and then give me feedback and I always could have done better.

Fortunately, the Tandem Topgrading Interview is amazingly robust. Both interviewers can make mistakes, but they cover for each other and in the end, rapport is very high, and the interviewers get terrific insights into the candidate.

Topgrading Hiring Step #9: Write a Draft Executive Summary

This is another "common sense" hiring step PCA software can embed – it's the rigor of systematically analyzing all the available hiring data and writing a draft executive summary.

> **Bet on people changing when they have proven they can change.**

Don't bet that you can change a candidate even if the candidate promises to do better. Topgraders routinely scrutinize 50 (yes, 50! ... yes, you can do it!) competencies. Experience over the years shows that some can be changed (green, below), some can't (red), and others are in-between.   Only bet a candidate will overcome weaker points when the Topgrading Interview shows a *long* pattern of overcoming weaker points.

Ease of Changing Competencies

Relatively Easy to Change	Harder, but Doable	Very Difficult to Change
Risk Taking	Judgment/Decision Making	Intelligence
Leading Edge	Strategic Skills	Analysis Skills
Education	Pragmatism	Conceptual Ability
Experience	Track Record	Creativity
Organization/Planning	Resourcefulness/Initiative	Integrity
Self-Awareness/Feedback	Excellence	Assertiveness
First Impression	Independence	Vision
Customer Focus	Stress Management	Inspiring Followership
Team Player	Adaptability	Energy/Drive
Communications - Oral	Likability	Enthusiasm/Passion
Communications - Written	Listening	Ambition
Political Savvy	Negotiation Skills	Tenacity
Selecting A Players	Persuasion	
Training/Development/Coaching	Team Builder	
Goal Setting	Change Leadership	
Empowerment	Conflict Management	
Performance Management	Compatibility of Needs	
Redeploying B/C Players	Balance in Life	
Diversity		
Running Meetings		

Topgrading Hiring Step #10: Ask Candidate to Arrange Reference Calls

Three decades ago I was devoting all my professional time to finding the very best practices in hiring and someone said, "Ask candidates to arrange the reference calls." I doubted that would work, since most companies prohibit their managers from accepting reference calls.

But it does work. High performers are *delighted* to ask former bosses and others to accept "personal" (not business) reference calls from a prospective employer. And 90% of former bosses accept the calls, knowing there is zero chance their former A player would sue them if they didn't get the job.

Note that there are more than two dozen Topgrading professionals, and not one of us has heard of even one legal or ethical incident arising from Step #10. (That goes for all of the Topgrading steps, by the way.)

So, for a mid-manager candidate, the Tandem Topgrading interviewers might ask the candidate to arrange personal reference calls with three former bosses, two former peers, and three former subordinates. The candidate does all the work (not HR recruiters!), and within two days the candidate emails, "Yes, they will all be happy to talk, and here are their mobile numbers and availability."

Topgrading Hiring Step #11: Coach Your New Hire!

Coaching a new hire is perhaps the most powerful and the easiest coaching a manager will do. With a huge amount of information about a newly-hired A player, what a shame it would be to wait for a routine annual performance appraisal to begin the coaching process.

With Topgrading, candidates are promised coaching within a couple of weeks for three purposes: 1) onboarding, 2) turbo-boost immediate performance, and 3) development for future positions.

The Tandem Topgrading interviewers simply meet with the new hire, and review their Executive Summary, and they already know that their A player has good self-awareness, recognizes strengths and areas for improvement, and probably already has a history of following through on Individual Development Plans (IDPs).

The Tandem Topgrading interviewers have done their "heavy lifting," so the hew hire is the one to absorb the feedback, ask questions, and carve out an IDP that addresses the three purposes. Easy!

And this is fun. With high levels of trust and mutual respect, and with a new hire eager to perform well, this coaching session is typically light-hearted, purposeful, and very productive.

Topgrading Hiring Step #12: Measure Hiring Success Annually

Many new Topgraders tend to think of this step as so far in the future that they don't need to think of it. But CEOs easily connect this step to Step #1 – measuring percent high performers hired (and promoted), and costs of mis-hires.

The purpose of it is major: it keeps the whole team focused on what is important: quality of talent hired and promoted. Without annual measurements fed back to the organization, Topgrading will be "just another program, a flavor of the month." Every successful Topgrading company integrates talent strategy with company strategy.

Topgrading drives superior talent, and that high-performing mindset becomes integral to the company culture, "part of our DNA," as is commonly stated.

How do you do those annual measurements? It can be simple or more complicated, but 1) estimate costs of every mis-hire, using the Topgrading Cost of Mis-Hire Form (Step #1), and 2) fill in the Topgrading success chart:

Showing this chart to managers once per year will reinforce Topgraders ("I'm doing it *right!*") and inspire laggards to embrace Topgrading.

CONCLUSION

These 12 Topgrading Steps will help you hire and promote better performers within your teams they will make your career soar, and your shareholders will be very pleased.

This book began with a typical hiring scenario. Let's revisit it, but show how Topgrading transforms "typical" to a much more effective process, with much better results:

Typical Hiring	Topgrading Hiring
Recruiters don't send good enough candidates	Your Virtual Bench produces many excellent, prescreened candidates
The resumes of candidates are usually incomplete and packed with hype	The Career History Form adds the facts you need to efficiently and effectively pre-screen candidates

Typical Hiring	Topgrading Hiring
Your interviews are not very revealing	The tandem Topgrading Interviews, using the Topgrading Interview Guide, are extremely revealing
Reference checks are generally worthless	Candidate-arranged reference calls are revealing and motivate the candidate to be honest in the interview
Too often the person hired disappoints you. Your results are: 25% High Performers Hired	Your results are: 90% High Performers Hired

Topgrading Methods

	Used	Not Fully Used
A Player Hired		
Non-A Player Hired		

Of all talent management practices, the single most important, by far, is hiring and promoting high performers. Companies consider themselves "Topgraders" when they have 75%-90% high performers. And they report that the other parts of talent management become relatively easy:

- Reducing turnover is a breeze when Topgrading assures a close-to-perfect job fit.

- Coaching high performers is fun; coaching underperformers is a pain.

- Succession planning is easy with a solid "bench."

And when entire companies soar in revenues and profits, growth opportunities open up, people earn more money, and as a bonus,

Topgraders have such strong teams they can delegate a lot and enjoy balance in life!

Topgrading Resources

Want to learn more? Please go to www.SmartTopgrading.com.

How to Get Started

1. Sign up for Topgrading Tips on the Home Page. This free 90-second read helps you implement Topgrading successfully.

2. Read (free) Press & Articles.

3. Get the forms Starter Kit . Try out the breakthrough Topgrading Career History Form and Topgrading Interview Guide. Use each just once and you'll see how costly mis-hires can be avoided.

More Advanced Topgrading Resources

1. Attend a two-day Topgrading Workshop. In addition to leaning the basics, you'll get the latest insights and case studies. With a 7-1 attendee-to-Topgrading professional ratio, you'll get all your questions answered.

2. Use the 7-Hour Topgrading Toolkit, to train your managers. The kit includes the classic Topgrading and other books, workbooks, audios of the DVD, and quarterly conference calls with me.

3. Invite a Topgrading professional to make a speech.

4. Use Topgrading professionals to conduct "second opinion" interviews of finalists for senior executive positions.

5. Use the best HR software, with the 12 Topgrading steps embedded. Contact us (Brad.Smart@Topgrading.com) for information.

How to Roll Out Topgrading in our Company

Scenarios are spelled out in simple terms, detailing how small and mid-sized companies typically roll out Topgrading with:

• in-house training

• licensed Topgrading forms and guides

Get Your Questions Answered

1. Email questions to Brad.Smart@Topgrading.com and we'll get back to you promptly.

2. Call 847-244-5544 and we'll talk in person.

We really do believe that Topgrading had a great deal to do with our success. And that for the American Heart Association doesn't just translate into the bottom line; that translates into saving more lives.

—Almarie Wagner, Executive Vice President,
American Heart Association

Brad's "second opinion" interviews and Topgrading tools have helped us pick the right executives, which is key to making money in private equity.

—Earl Powell, Founding Partner and Chairman Emeritus,
Trivest Partners, L.P.

Topgrading has definitely helped the company's overall performance. The tandem chronological interview is the best approach I know of for picking high performers, and we use it for external hires and internal promotions.

—Curt Clawson, President, CEO, and Chairman,
Hayes Lemmerz, International

Having read the book several years ago, I was intrigued. Now after implementing Topgrading for all new hires and promotions, I am thrilled. Our organization has embraced the philosophy and process and we are seeing the results.....the right people in the right positions.

—Timothy T. Tevens, President and CEO,
Columbus McKinnon Corporation

Our executives and customers rave about how the Topgrading interview tools and processes consistently swing the odds in favor of selecting only high performers.....resulting in innovation, incremental revenue, and increased operating income throughout the enterprise.

—John H. Dickey, Sr. Vice President,
Hillenbrand Industries, Inc.
and Hill-Rom Company

When I look back at the dramatic success of our company, I can clearly point to the implementation of Topgrading as the pivotal moment that made our success possible. I implore every business owner to make Topgrading mandatory in their company. A Topgraded team is the ultimate secret weapon to crush the competition.

—Richard Rossi, Co-Chairman,
EnvisionEMI